By
Ocean
Divided

Poems of Ireland and New England

Kevin V. Moore

Copyright © 2013 Kevin V. Moore
All rights reserved.

ISBN: 1481920545
ISBN-13: 9781481920544

For Mary

Table of Contents

Of Ireland	1
A Beltane Prayer	3
An Gorta Mor	4
Arrival, Grosse Ile	6
Basic Economics 1847	7
Beith	9
Bits	10
Blessing for Old Age	12
Commission to Inquire into Child Abuse	13
Christians	14
Cleansing	15
Daley and Halligan	16
Fionn Mac Cumhail	18
For Bride at Imbolc	19
For Tara's Dead	20
Guardians	21
Heritage	23
I Beg a Favor	25
In Memoriam	27
In Nomine Patris	29
Into the Unknown	30
John O'Donohue	32
Migration	33
Patrick Joseph O'Connell	34
Post-Famine	35
Poulnabrone Dolman	37
Prayer Beneath the Oak	38
Praying	40
Questlings	41
Siobhan	42

Sweeping	43
The Cost of Dying	44
The Death of Conlaoch	45
The Elders	47
The Epistle of St. Patrick	49
The Hound	50
The Magdalenes	51
The Ritual	53
The Solstice	55
The Waking	56
Of New England	59
A Dream	61
A Winter Prayer	62
Almost	63
Aspirations	64
Bleeah!	65
Californication	66
Katharsis	67
In the Cemetery	68
Change	69
Cohabitation	70
Coke Kilns	71
Crossing the Veldt	73
The Crow	75
For Barbaro	77
Forest Mourning	78
I Know You	79
King Phillip and I	80
Ladybug	82
Life Cycles	84
The Nature of Man	85
Pond Life	86
Post Mortem	87
Senior Slain in Shop Setting	88
Snow Fence	90

Sugaring	91
The Adventure	92
The Altar Boy's Lament	93
The Challenge	95
The Closet Naturist	97
The Fabric Mill	98
The Horse-Draw	100
The Search	101
The Sun	102
The Wall	103
The Weesit	104
To Emily	106
Tobacco	107
Veteran's Day	109
Viet Nam	110
Why The Sky is Blue	111

PART 1

Of Ireland

A Beltane Prayer

Choruses of meadowlarks
encourage the mayflowers
and merry buttercups.
Even the surly nettle
seeks the sun.
The sheep and cattle
revel in the old meadow
now made new.
The trees, embarrassed
at being seen naked,
hastily cover themselves.
Shadowy trout swim
again where ice
had forced their sleep.
In this sun-touched valley
let all who witness
this joyous rebirth
raise their faces
to the sun
and sing praises to
the Gods of Summer.

An Gorta Mor

1851
Una, last child of
her mother, packs her
few things to leave.
She wears her mother's
wedding ring, unusual,
with both gold and silver
interwoven.
"Tis but for the unknown",
her mother said.
"If ye need it not, won't
it return with ye, then?"
And, through tears, Una
leaves Tuar Mhic Eadaigh
behind her.

Three weeks later, the
ring is all of value
she retains
as she boards the Avon.

1851
The ship Avon, under
Capt. Elijah Dickinson
has moored at Grosse Isle
Quebec, Canada.

She carries 241 passengers
requiring quarantine,
and Bond in the amount
of £241 has been made.
The Avon reports 36
marked Lost in Transit,
buried at sea.

2.

1852
Capt. Elijah Dickinson,
having completed his contract,
has returned to
his home and family
in Southampton, England.

Among other gifts he
brings to his wife
is a ring, unusual,
with gold and silver
interwoven.

Arrival, Grosse Ile

At the mouth
of the St. Lawrence,
sixty-five days
out of Liverpool.
The travel is slow,
too many waiting.
Food is brought
from shore
for those that can
afford it, or even
keep it down.
For the first time
below-decks is
cleaned, awaiting
Health Inspection.
The Quarantine Boats
shuttle the sick
and dying,
for many, their
final ride.
God grants them
the favor of
being too ill
to know they die
within sight of
freedom.

Basic Economics 1847

The trees were all gone.
At least of size enough
for masts and spars,
or single keel.
The Colonies were rife
with them, though.
Sail West, empty, save
for ballast to raise
the waterline,
unload the ballast,
load the wood and
return.
No profit in bringing
stones to Canada,
they have plenty there.

Then the canny Captains
found weight that would
load and unload itself,
and pay for the privilege.
Pack in the living, sail West,
and those left alive would
unload themselves,
making room for the long timbers.

{ continued }

Other than dying for the Queen,
in battles not of their making,
the next best use for
the Irish.

Beith
(Birch)

"Look at me" says the birch,
standing out, outstanding,
when all the others
hide in the night.
Stark, fluorescent,
in the sheer moon's light.
I light the path for
those who follow trees,
They who walk the
Sacred Path
once trodden by the gods.
"Look at me"
says the birch.

Bits

In the Burren,
where the wind harries
the scant soil,
bits of a skull appear,
like shells on some
rock-strewn shore.
Dropped there by
sated raven,
or scattered by
iron axe.
Little does it matter
to the original owner,
he is away,
searching for
Tir na nOg.
What dreams escaped,
when this vault
was opened?
Who remembered his
not returning?
Did some woman
rend her hair
and keen into the fire?
It matters not
to the original owner,
she can't be heard
from Tir na nOg.

Were there sons
to bear his name,
to pick up the
dropped tools and
work the land?

2.

Or did he simply
disappear, without
a trace, without mourning
an eternity searching
for Tir na nOg.

Blessing for Old Age

May the warmth of
summer sun be on
your cheek,
and the throat-closing cold
of spring water be there
to slake your thirst.
May a well laid thatch
protect you from rain
and Brigit's hearth keep
off the damp.
May you gain the respect
of your neighbors
and may you have the love
of your children
and their children.
May you have a loyal dog
to sit at your feet
and a soft chair
to give you rest.
May someone you love
bring you a bottomless
cup of The Waters of Life,
to help you contemplate the day,
and plan for the morrow.

Commission to Inquire into Child Abuse

Consecrate, celebrate,
celibate and deviate,
They arbitrate for God
and procreation, yet
know neither.
Now exposed as
the worst possible
in loco parentis
their answer is
"but not all",
as if small innocence
overcomes great evil.
It is your turn
to kneel and take
the stick, and
even that won't
suffice.
I pray the Hell
you promised
is even worse
than you
imagined.

Christians

The tonsured ones
in coarse robes
of brown
came first alone
and then with
men of the tuath.
They drove the wise ones
from the grove
and cut down the oaks.
They heaped the once
proud sentinels into
the circle of stones
and lit the fire.
They thought that
would bring us
to their god.
As if our gods
could be killed
by axe or fire.
We stood away
from the heat and flame,
stunned that this god
they offered us
needed man to
strike for him.

Cleansing

The burning thatch winks
in the smoke-choked air.
Heat, in this dreary dawn.
The despised Magistrate
and his sycophantic slaveys
turn another household out.
Hardly time to grab the crucifix,
beads, and small things.
The tiny vial of Holy Water
boils on the mantle.
Surely, such evil
is a black sin. Why,
then, doesn't God strike them?
Is it too, a sin, to pray
Him to do so?
The horses slip and shy
from the keening and
the waves of heat.
One rider is unseated.
He quickly remounts,
embarrassed to be seen
by such as those
whose lives he has
just destroyed.

Daley and Halligan
(Hanged in Northampton, Massachusetts, June 5, 1806)

Why would it
come as a surprise?
To Domenic Daley
and James Halligan,
immigrants, aliens,
exiles,
Irish and Papists,
as if simply being Irish
wasn't enough.
Falsely accused,
wrongfully jailed,
laughingly tried,
and righteously hanged.
Stern Yankees by the score
filled the streets
to catch a glimpse
of these monsters.
Robbery and murder
called for harsh and
swift, if incomplete, justice.
But do not cry
that the citizens of Northampton
are without mercy.
Give them their heathen priest,
and then our Christian hemp.

Nothing new to these
Sons of Erin,
the only oddity
is that it is not
an English hand that springs
the trap.

Fionn Mac Cumhail

How can I have been slain
by hawthorn barb
yet skin unbroken?
Am I the Rígfénnid Fionna
Protector to the Ard Ri,
undefeated in battle,
master of the Sword Dance
and cannot rise?
The Tuatha seek their revenge
but dare not meet me, sword-to-sword.
Seek, Bran!, Seek Sceolaun!,
find again my being, my Sive.
Cry out when the scent
is in the air and
I will rise and come to you
through the mist of the Sídhe,
the hole in my heart
sealed by love.

For Bride at Imbolc

Brighid, Bridey, never bride
Triple Goddess
Join our fire.
Daughter of Dagda and Dubthach both.
Goddess Saint Midwife Healer
Join our fire.
Muse of poets
Keeper of fire
Join us that we may
Honor thee.

Spread your magic cloak
O'er Kildare's ground
There your healing well be found
Be well, well be
Light brilliant and profound
Tend we the fire
These nineteen days
That you attend
This Holy Day.

For Tara's Dead

I was called Boarkiller, when I died,
here on blesséd Tara's side,
A Norse axe destroyed my face,
I drowned in blood, in this same place.
Since that day I have here lain,
and thought forever would remain.

But now machines that rape the earth
Demean my death, and shame my birth.
The saddest thing, what galls the most,
Is not this grave of fallen host,
For we died in Honor, at Honor's hand,
The Norse and we both loved the land.

And now again, as we here mould,
Our sons will kill us, loving gold.
Mark me well, my ill-bred spawn,
There's more here than you've counted on.
Seven times seven will curse their race
If these bones are torn from my dying place.

Guardians

Close your eyes
and follow the path
that ends at self.
Look on all sides
at those who shelter
you from wind, sun,
rain, snow, evil.
They stand for you
in your time of need,
on your journey
to discovery.
Over-stretching, encircling
a living thatch above,
placed there by
those you only
hope to know.
For unknown reasons
you are important
to them. They
see reason to keep
you safe, reasons
that you have not
yet discovered.
Suit your life to
honor and thank them,
a symbiotic relationship

{ continued }

that pleases both.
Though they will
vanish as you open
your eyes to the world
around you,
they will be there
for you always,
as you follow
the path.

Heritage

Where are you going,
my child, boy of mine,
To school for to learn,
oh mother, my mother,
And what will you learn,
my child, son of mine,
All there is to know,
my mother, dear mother,
And what will you do
with this knowledge,
dear son, son of mine,
My true love I'll find,
oh mother, sweet mother,
And then we will marry,
oh mother of mine.
What will you do with her,
young man, son of mine,
We will have children,
dear mother, like you did,
dear mother of mine.
And how will you keep them,
dear son, man of mine,
I'll follow the drum,
oh mother, my mother,
and take up the gun,
sweet mother of mine,

{ continued }

and I'll die to protect them,
oh mother, sad mother,
Just like my father,
oh mother of mine.

I Beg a Favor

Cloak me in the warmth
of the sun
Pry my sealed eyes open
to the greening
Waken my loins to the
rut of the Stag
Deafen me with the bronze
trumpet of rebirthing
Lift me from Winters icy
burial chamber
where I have lain
dormant and asleep
Cast me laughing and
naked down the steep
hill of flowers
Make me scream in delight
at the beauty
the Gods have spread
before me
Drown me in Spring Mead
revive me with the red lips
of womanhood
and the breath of promise
Strike flint from my wretched bones
and relight the fires
of new beginning.

{ continued }

For my entire existence
I have awaited this
moment.

In Memoriam

Warmed by the fire,
whiskey in hand,
it's safe to mourn
that once dead land,
where generations died
short years ago,
though some would
say it wasn't so,
that learnéd men
of modern race
could starve their brethren
with such planned grace
and see the blight
bleed o'er the ground
where gentle shamrock
now is found.
But that was then,
and this is now,
bright machines now
pull the plow,
"It was the times"
they say, "no
harm intended".
"Those times are gone,

{ continued }

the blight has ended."
I fill my glass,
and say "Not yet".
I'll ne'er forgive,
I'll ne'er forget.

In Nomine Patris

I was afraid of him.
The long black dress
with all the buttons.
Sometimes he would come
to dinner,
when we had ham.
They were honored
that I was chosen
to learn to serve God.
Cassock and surplice
and memorization.
And other things
that I can't tell them.
I saw him today
at the courthouse,
in ordinary clothes.
He is old now, and I'm
still afraid of him,
but
I'm more afraid
of myself.

Into the Unknown

He went away
at lambing,
though the sheep
were years in
the past.
"Find a Priest",
he was told,
"they will write
that you are safe".
I will find one here,
if they, too, haven't
gone across.
The embrace,
the tears and
the loneliness.

In black shadows,
in reeking pestilence,
in fever that
erases thought,
he struggles to
remember.
And finally, when
the time comes,
he asks for

a Priest.
Not to bless,
but to write
and he will slide
into the sea,
with neither Rites
nor writing.

John O'Donohue
R.I.P.
January 3, 2008

No colorful scarves,
team colors,
in the slim ranks
of the Philosopher-Poets.
Yet when an icon
falls, how greater
the loss.
Not tries or goals,
but seeds,
sown in like minds
to grow and flourish
and produce
soul-changing visions,
new awareness,
the touch of
the Gods.
Only a small part
of the world will
mourn him,
but the intensity of
his passing
leaves all of
humankind, sadly
lacking.

Migration

Cobbles of white bone
pave the sea floor
from Erin to America.
Scattered amongst
their paleness lie
the hopes of a generation.
Committed here by
cruel and craven Captains
chosen by uncaring Crown,
a carrion causeway of
consigned corpses,
callow and cold.
Forget them never!
Lest, with that
final indignity, they
will rise from that
unfathomable depth,
they will finish
their intended journey
from Hell to Hope
and back again
and icily stare out at you
from your frosted mirror.

Patrick Joseph O'Connell
1878-1950

My mother's father, "P.J.",
was a tailor.
I don't know if
he ever had a shop
of his own.
He had a route
of clothing stores
where he would
do the alterations,
hem the trousers,
shorten sleeves,
replace buttons
and drink.
Old family legend
has it that
he once hit
"The Numbers Pool"
and rode the Club Car
between Northampton
and Boston
until the money
ran out.
Lucky for him,
it ran out in
Northampton,
where he lived
and drank.

Post-Famine
1850-1900

In the aftermath
of the great diaspora,
they were seen as
retarded children
who could not
feed themselves.
Fit only for
digging in the dirt
along rail-beds and
in coal mines,
in dusty mills,
these Sons and Daughters
of Eriu, slaves,
domestics, and
day-laborers, when
there was no horse
nor machine to be had.
But these souls,
these believers in
indomitable hope,
survived.
And these global orphans,
having seen the signs
"No Irish Need Apply",
applied, indeed.

{ continued }

Soon, the FitzGeralds,
the Flahertys, O'Connells
and O'Neills, with
all their kith and kin,
had learned to
feed themselves.
Yet even in placing
the silk glove

2.

on the calloused hand,
they clung to their past,
to their lost green land,
to their Irishness.

Poulnabrone Dolman
Co. Clare

The shiny American children
want to climb atop
the Dolman.
"You can take our pitchers, Ma!"
The shiny American mother
appears to acquiesce.
Though American myself
(not very shiny)
I say "it's against the law".

Secretly, I wish for
an Iron Age warrior
to cleave them all
with his shiny sword
and then to finish
in the car-park where
the shiny American father
sits and drums his fingers.

Prayer Beneath the Oak

In the vast shadow,
generations of forest-dwellers
have sought food
and shelter.
I, too, seek shelter
and sustenance,
but of a different sort,
beneath your blesséd bows.
Speak to me, Oak,
for you are nearer
to the gods,
and speak to them, Oak,
on my humble behalf.
Become my priest;
my messenger,
tell them I am trying
to understand their ways,
ask them, mighty totem,
to show me
the Way, along
this misty/mystic path.
Allow me to rest
within your sacred circle,
trusting completely
in your goodness
and strength.
And let me, like

the other creatures
that worship here,
leave refreshed
and sated.

Praying

The gods are vain
and proud;
they accept man's respect
as their due.
Prayers to them are
like flakes of snow
unnoticed in the drifts.
If you wish to gain
their hearing,
think you are their equal.
That hubris will appear
as a distant flame
in deep darkness,
pausing their revelry
and time will cease
its passing,
the sun will blacken
and the moon disappear.
Your breath will alternate
fire and ice, and
your bowels will loosen.
Now that you have
their attention,
make your request.

Questlings

They come to me and say
"So you're a Druid?"
And perhaps they have
heard good things.
And they next say
"Can you make me
a Druid?"
And in their eyes I see
a pitiable want, as if
with some oaken twig I
could change their lives.
They are unwilling to
spend the life-long study,
the endless meditations,
the self-examinations,
the thousands of conversations
and arguments
and always, the books.
They think I am the
Wal-Mart of Inner Peace
and Understanding,
where all they need to know
is "Small, Medium,
or Large".

Siobhan

"I'll put down *Sally*...
you won't need that
other name here, girl,
you're in America, now,
no dirt floored cottages
in the city."
At the door, hucksters
lined up like cattle
buyers, eyeing
the latest to arrive.
Irish themselves,
they have found
a niche,
buying and selling
their countrymen.
The fortunate will find
domestic work,
cooking, cleaning,
endless scrubbing
of the priceless
wooden floors,
when clay only
required a quick
sweep-up.

Sweeping

The wind comes
after the battle,
drying sightless eyes,
guiding the ravens
to their spoils.
Magically, it cools
the dead
and warms the dying,
it carries shouts
of victory and of
last words,
touching all
equally,
victor and vanquished.
As a child gathering
berries, the wind
gathers names, souls,
rushing off to inform
those not present,
of their loss.
Slowly, it erases
the bits of human being
until all that is left
is the tatters, rags,
the myths,
and then the wind
moves on.

The Cost of Dying

At night the steel-wheeled wagon comes,
Horse's hooves like tinny drums,
Flickering torches yellow light,
One more has gone into the night.
The crepe will hang upon the morrow,
Black suits aired out, and chairs to borrow.
Some food will come in iron pot,
Small whiskey bottles will be bought,
They had a cow. The last around,
To pay the cost of Holy Ground,
But others, not a penny raise
To pay the cost to end their days.
O'Brian, then, no wagon comes,
Nor iron shoes will play the drums,
No Priest to fetch the water Blessed,
No whiskey jar to ease his rest,
And out behind the fallen shed,
New widow from her fevered bed,
With broken mattock digs the hole,
Just deep enough to sheathe his soul,
And from the wall she lays a stone,
Keening, softly, sick, alone.

The Death of Conlaoch

In a torrid blue-green rage
the air intense with flame,
The Hound in sparking anger
Curses Aoife's name.
The Ulstermen, a-tremble,
the Gods will hold their breath,
As wrapped in battle-fury,
Cuchulain mourns the young son's death.
From Dun Scathach came the warrior,
to Ulster's troubled land,
To meet Dun Dealgan's Hound there,
and to fall beneath his hand.
The arc of the Gae Bulga,
never erring, ever true,
Famous name to none-at-all,
the deadly missile flew.
And in death the ges is lifted,
and Conlaoch's name is said,
Cuchulain's ring upon the hand
of the only son, now dead.
Conchubar, the Ulster King,
provoked and deep in fear,
knows the battle-fury's dangers,
and calls his Druid near,
Cathbad, on his order,
lays a spell upon the land,

{ continued }

creating unknown foes
on the sands at Baille's Strand.
And there three days and nights,
sword thrusts against the tide,
the vengeful fury rages,
until Cuchulain's fury died.

2.

Cuchulain curses Aoife's name
and for his only son he weeps,
on the sands at Baille's Strand,
at last, the spent Hound sleeps.

The Elders

What will become
of the believers?
Those who starved
to make their tithe,
who washed altar cloths
and fed himself
on Sundays.
What of the dim
gray building with
light stopping windows
bought by the
well-to-do.
What of those who
married and buried
and knelt under The Hound
your laws?
More for the Missions,
above and beyond,
the Organ Fund,
Special Collections,
the new Cadillac.
All they have left
is the most extreme
of unctions,

{ continued }

the Rites.
Will you whisper
to them in your Latin
"It was all a joke"?

The Epistle of St. Patrick

"Special Collection",
you say, "for
mounting costs",
and wasn't it
the mounting then
that's costing now?
Thirty percent
decline in members
and Himself,
in Rome, says
"We must continue
to travel the hard road",
Hard road, indeed,
with enough spent
on robes, hats,
and red shoes
to feed dozens...
(and with the
Clergy Discount).
The Celtic Tiger
shakes itself
and the fleas
cast off all
wear The Collar.
Even the blind
man sees the dawn.

The Hound

Oh, to be the warrior's dog,
Beside the chariot wheels to jog
De-spelling mist and Druid-fog,
The proud hound of the Hound.

To dodge and dance as arrows fly
With snarls and nips as we pass by
We can't be bested, he and I
The brave hound and the Hound.

And when the battle-furies fled
Lay by and clean the jaws of red
Gaze across the sea of dead
The good hound and the Hound.

Arise and leave this killing-place
To see again sweet Emer's face
And rest by fires warming grace
Weary hound sleeps near the Hound.

No better life for dog or man
Than Honor serve and foe withstand
To live or die as Gods command
To be Cuchulain's hound..

The Magdalenes

In the bright summer
of my fourteenth year,
The Priest and Father
brought me here,
They said "to curb
my sinful ways",
to learn to work
and God to praise,
I had already
learned to hurt,
for letting Jimmy
up my skirt,
the same skirt laid
across my back
as Da applied
the paddywhack,
me Ma brought salve,
and towels, iced,
and dried my tears
and spoke of Christ.

Then came the Priest
and we're away,
with "you'll come home,
repent and pray".

{ continued }

That summer, then,
within me died
and many more
I've passed inside,
no sun, nor warmth,
no joyous hope,
my youth, my life,
washed out in soap.

2.

Each Morning Prayers
I pray to die,
But too afraid
to take the lye,
For faint belief,
to take my life,
would only cause
post mortal strife,
The only promise
left is one--
to rest in Heaven
when I'm done,
but even this
celestial plan,
depends, Ochone,
upon a man.

The Ritual

The fire pushes
back the veil,
hissing, gnarling,
through the pale,
with pleas to gods
we wait the dawn,
seeing wisps
of those now gone.
We ask their presence,
yet stand struck dumb
lest the dead might
truly come,
and mock us
for our mewling praise
and jeer us for
our worldly ways,
and find us, wanting,
thin-blooded, weak,
without true fire,
born to seek.
Age-old questions
fill ones head,
no sudden insight
from the dead,

{ continued }

This knowledge, you
will ne'er acquire,
'til standing here,
...beyond the fire.

The Solstice

On the Winter Solstice
at Newgrange,
the rising sun
flows through
the portal and
shines on the
altar stone.
So then,
let it shine
into your heart,
re-kindling your
spirit,
in preparation
for the journey
back to light.
Each day, may
your inner fire
grow stronger,
every dawn, may
the day grow longer,
and may you one day
dance at
Beltane
again.

The Waking

Moments after the Priest
has closed the door,
the women of the village
appear, bearing warm
dishes wrapped in cloths.
"I'm so sorry for your loss".
Tea, cakes, and
the laying out.
Later, the men arrive,
ill-suited, reeking of
shaving soap
and whiskey.
Soon the cottage
is unbearable
with the heat and
smoky overcrowding,
all the stove burners lit,
Holy candles in the
viewing room.
In unwritten tradition
the men will depart
to the barn or shed
where a drop might
be found.
Late arrivals will be
dismembered in whispers
by the sitting women.

In this time-honored
Christian barbarism,
the only comfortable soul
belongs to the
guest of honor.

PART 2

Of New England

A Dream

I dreamt of
the librarian
last night, and
woke regretting
it.
Not for the
dream itself,
but for buying
into the cinematic
stereotype,
just because
she is pretty
and wears
glasses.
In the dream
she kept them
on.
Now I'll have
to leave my
returns in the
Night Drop
until the
dream fades.

A Winter Prayer

Paint me with sun, Gods,
for I am rigid with cold.
This poor frame is shaky,
the mortises dried
and loose,
the belly-fire
snoored to ash.
Like an old barn,
the years abuse
have left me leaning
and away from plumb.
Winter is too long now,
the cold blue shades
reflect my infirmities,
but,
give me one sign,
however faint, that
Spring will return,
and creaking and shifting,
with your blessings,
I will maintain.

Almost

At the height
of love-making,
when the colors
seem to brighten
and sound throbs
like a too fast
beating heart,
all the senses teeter
at the lip of
the abyss.
I hesitate,
at tactile overdose,
gleaning every tiny
atom
before the crash.
And the slow
return to rest
in damp embrace
is almost, almost,
almost,
as good.

Aspirations

My mother had a
plan, you see,
to make a fine
young priest
of me.

She probably thought
I wasn't listenin',
she should
have specified
a "Christian".

Bleeah!

Not like Marat,
in the tub,
nor Caesar,
on the steps,
but upon the couch,
plucking at the
coverlet,
I will pass,
laid low by
unseen enemies
within.
Pale and gone
amidst
bouquets of
used tissues and
sticky spoons.
The drone of
talking football heads
chants my dirge.
Set this poor pallet
onto a raft
and give me
the Viking Rites,
Weeping Women
sing
"One Flu Over
the Cuckoo's Nest".

Californication

Something I recently bought
had a warning label on it
that said "This product has been
found to cause cancer by
the State of California".

Are the other forty-nine
immune or do they
just not care?
When I was a child,
California may as well
have been on the moon,
not a place I might go.

As an adult, that
hasn't changed.
California should have
a label of it's own
"This state has been found
to cause madness
by the rest of the world."

San Andreas should not
be a fault, but a reality.
It would be their
first taste of it..

Katharsis

I have never
been comfortable on
my knees, neither
metaphorically nor
physically. It is
worse with the feel
of your small foot
upon my nape.
Were the position
of my choosing
I might acquiesce
and do penance
but the beads will
never touch my hand.
Not even sorrow
comes to me.
Blinded in your quest
it seems ironic
that you truly don't
know who you are
nor what you
have done.
I will rise to
my feet
unassisted.

In the Cemetery

Three men, leaning on
a red truck, drinking coffees.
The apparent boss steps
forward as I approach.
"Is there a plot-map
for this cemetery?",
I ask. "How far back
do you want to go?"
he replies.
"Early nineteen-hundreds",
my answer. "Nope,
mapping started in
fifty-one", he says.
Seeing disappointment,
he offers "What names?".
"O'Connell and Murphy"
The helpers snicker and smile.
"From that big oak, all
the way to the fence,
and then all the way
to the road", he gestures,
"mostly Murphys and O'Connells."
"Help yourself".
I walk away wondering
how often they get a
chance to laugh here.

Change

It was summer
when I went to bed
and Fall woke me,
rudely,
in the morning.
There's more comfort
in getting warm,
than to wake
basted, like a turkey,
in self-made gravy.
Though no fan
of Winter's coming,
perhaps this year
I can accept it,
gracefully,
thankful to be alive
to note its arrival.

Cohabitation

We are joined
by things shared.
Yours and mine
somehow became ours.
Yet I sometimes
long for something
to be mine alone,
perhaps a secret,
buried treasure,
not to share.
Not to return to
mine alone
but to savor
in solitary times,
a return to selfishness
and immaturity
that came before you.
I won't ask for
your understanding,
and that will be
my secret.

Coke Kilns
Leverett, Massachusetts

The kilns stand empty.
Ivy betrays their lack
of fire.
Inside, the odor
of charcoal remains.
Twenty cord of
slab lumber,
unusable for any
legitimate construct
stacked against the
walls until filled.
The smoke-hole
is tempered with
wet mud.
It is now up to
the old man,
who touches it off.
Time to dig at
bark splinters and wait.
If "she flares", all
can "go up in smoke"
stones cracking and
nothing left but ash.
If all goes well,
pungent black charcoal,
now needing to be

{ continued }

bagged and sold,
money gone before
the black stain washes off.

For Pete Glazier

Crossing the Veldt

When I was sixteen,
I never thought of death
until it visited my father.
Even then, I considered
it an aberration;
no one else my age
had a dead father.
When it came back
for my mother,
I was hardly surprised,
she had been
rehearsing for years.
Forty years pass.
I live in a herd
of wildebeests.
The lions get Elvis,
John Kennedy,
Marilyn Monroe,
but those of us
in the middle of
the pack run on.
Ten more migrations
and I find myself,
flanks scarred, on the
edge of the crowd,
limping slightly.

{ continued }

Away in the yellow grass
a young, fast, lion notices.

The Crow

Wonderfully adapted
is our crow,
who sits above
the traffic flow,
like gourmet diners
read their menus,
he scans the list
of asphalt venues,
and spying squirrel
that ran too slow,
he calls the furry
feast below.
With his brethren
he will dine
on flattened fauna,
tender and sublime
and you may wonder,
stop to think
how they manage
on the brink,
dodging traffic
whizzing by,
yet never see the
odd crow die?

{ continued }

As two or three
dine on tartare,
another watches,
to cry, CAR!, CAR!

For Barbaro
(put down Jan.29, 2007)

Good on ye!, Brave lad.
It's done, now.
I raise my glass to ye!
Oh, didn't ye just show them,
and how they roared.
But all for nowt.
What of the soft green pastures
and the mares?
Gone.
But, at least, so is
the pain.
They promised everything
and this is the result.
You gave them your love,
your trust,
and they lied.
You gave them your
legs and your heart,
and in that, died.
Ah, brave lad, of course
they lied,
It's what separates humans
from
horses.

Forest Mourning

The frost becomes dew
as the sun paints the forest.
The doe rises from her bed,
scenting, nostrils large.
Ears erect, she seeks
discordant sounds
signaling danger.
Steam rises from her back
and from the nest that
served her in sleep.
She tests each leg in turn,
arches her long neck,
preparing to move
to the grazing area.
Still alert, she steps
tentatively from the
dense laurel thicket.
Suddenly, a foreign sound,
which, had she recognized it,
would have saved her.
The bow string stops its hum
just as the arrow stops
her heart.
She will not be visiting
the grazing meadow today,
but elsewhere in the forest
life will go on unchanged.

I Know You

Where was it
that we met?
Long past time
unknown as yet,
How many lives ago
did this take place
when first you caused
my heart to race,
I feel you feel
but must deny
this misted tryst
from time gone by,
though mortal changes
different faces,
it's heart and soul
my love embraces.
Take my hand
by sky above,
enduring ever,
my one true love.

King Phillip and I

Atop Mount Sugarloaf,
once called "the-head-of-
the-great-beaver",
I sit where King Phillip sat.
I imagine wood canoes
on the riverbank below.
My mind cannot erase
the monuments to progress
before me, starting with
the concrete span
near the canoes.
In the distant haze,
the cement towers,
cellphone antennae,
asphalt, water tanks,
and even the tobacco nets
rectangular white stain.
I have no desire to time-travel,
too comfortable sitting in
the late autumn sun.
But if I did, and came across
the long-dead chief,
we would have no
common understanding.

And if he traveled to
where I now sit,
he would probably
say "How?".

*"Ladybug, ladybug
fly away home,
your house is on fire
an your chillrens alone."*

(Old Childrens Rhyme)

Ladybug

The ladybugs have
wintered at my house,
gangs of them
hidden, they think,
in ceiling corners.
Now that it is
February, occasionally
they will send out
a scout, checking
weather and traffic.
No, not Spring yet.
It saw its shadow,
so six more weeks
of Winter.
Back in their
colorful clutch
they turn their
collective backs
to the light,
commiserating with

each other about
house fires in
the past.

Life Cycles

The crow's claxon calls
announce clearly,
that the cat has
exited the barn.
The barn swallows
celebrate with
athletic aerobatics.

Above it all,
though below,
the cat ignores
the noise
as she slips
into the hay-field
in search of quieter,
more well-behaved prey.

Who will tell the cat
that the mowing-machine
is hunting prey
of its own?

The Nature of Man

Long aromatic brown lines
bisect the farmer's field
as the manure spreader
clatters along its route.
Unused nutrients returned
to whence they came.
Today, as I pass,
a massive flock
of Canada Geese
lined up for smorgasbord.
They don't migrate like
they used to, anymore.
The river never freezes
and they winter here.
Like the Parking Lot Gulls,
we have altered them.
They've re-invented themselves
to suit our ways.
While the Canadas dine on
cattle waste, the gulls
fight over Mac-fries.
Man lives in harmony
with nature...
but it's an ugly tune.

Pond Life

The frog takes all his meals with water,
A toad won't wash up when he oughta,
A salmon licks his chops and dines
On frog legs, though eschewing wines,
The eagle perched in lofty tree,
Without complaint will eat all three.

Post Mortem

I will not be buried
in a corporeal landfill
of the semi-righteous,
stone marking my
length of living,
rather barbecued in toto
until past well-done
mere dusty bits
perhaps scattered on
an icy sidewalk
to prevent others
from slipping into
my new world
prematurely.
My last good deed?
That piece of me
ethereal, having
left before the blaze
snickers, saying
"No, your
first."

Senior Slain in Shop Setting

The old woman in front
of me in line
smells of sawdust.
Perhaps somewhere
in her flowered torso
there's a leak,
and her stuffing is
falling out, perhaps
she's been to the
coffin-makers for
a fitting.
I wince as the clerk
announces "That'll be
thirteen-forty-seven".
Only then does the
spotted claw go into
the worn bag,
(as if today, paying for
groceries was a
new invention).
I know what lies ahead.
How badly do I need
this milk?
"Eleven, twelve, thirteen"
and then the wallet
is restored and the
tiny snapped purse

comes out.
The clerk senses my unease,
gives me an eye-roll.
"Thirty-five, forty"
and then the fatal
"forty-one...."

Snow Fence

The double row of cornstalks,
tan against the winter snow.
"How Clever!", I thought.
An organic snow fence
in lieu of the ugly, orange,
petroleum-based plastic.
The Yankee simplicity of it
forced me to inquire...
"Snow fence?" he said
"Too wet last fall
to run the chopper."
So much for ingenuity.

Sugaring
Conway, Massachusetts

The spiles and buckets
are mostly gone.
Bright polyethylene hose
loops from tree to tree
terminating in the
lowest spot to
yellow fiberglass tank.
The Currier and Ives horses
have been replaced
by shiny four-by-four
stereo vomiting noise
to cover the sound
of the electric pump.
It is a one almost-man
operation now,
the hip-hopping driver
wears dirty athletic shoes.
The syrup can't possibly
taste the same.

The Adventure

Soon enough, we'll sally forth,
My good friend Finn and I,
Exploring banks of frozen snow,
Where buried treasures lie.
He marks his passing faithfully,
Signed in yellow ink.
A message to his canine mates,
saying "Finn was here", I think.
Limited by length of leash,
His interest starts to flag,
Then, quickly, circles in the snow,
I'll have to use the bag.
That trace removed,
Our task is done,
And homeward bound are we.
Old man and dog enjoying life
When Finn goes out to pee.

The Altar Boy's Lament

It was The Stations of the Cross,
a rare non-Sunday Mass,
In the chapel of St. Monica
With a censer made of brass.
Father Mickey gave me charcoal,
And helped me give it light,
Frankincense to put on top,
"Make sure you get it right!",
"Don't put in too wee a bit,
or it won't last 'til done",
I picked a chunk that looked okay,
The same size as my thumb.
I was quite excited
To hold the Sacred Chain,
My Ma had trimmed my surplice
So I wouldn't trip (again).
Chanting, we began the rite,
Station One, then on to Two,
Plaster saints upon the wall,
Slowly fade from view.
By Six and Seven, they're all gone,
I can barely see the floor,
Soft coughing sounds have started now,
But I bravely swing some more.
We're up to Nine (I think we are),

{ continued }

Father Mickey's voice is cold,
In my ear comes a whisper,
"I'll deal with you", I'm told.
Some ushers opened windows,
And the haze was soon abated,
As I headed to the Sacristy,
Where Father Mickey waited.

2.

He boxed my ears, and pulled my hair,
And said I'm bound for Hell,
So I in turn punched Seamus,
Said "Next time I'll take the bell"!

The Challenge
Brimfield, Massachusetts

In the shade
above the meadow
where the water runs
cold all year-round,
King Trout waits.
Hooked and lost
two years running,
he mocks me.
Where the tree roots
overhang the pool,
an impossible cast,
a miss is fatal.
Thin line parts with
the fly remaining
stuck in bark.
One try, perhaps,
line jerks taut
bamboo bends
heart jumps, try
to stay cool.
Left, right, left, left,
wet aerobatics,
one foot in the water,
I use the net.
I close my eyes
imagining the crisp skin

{ continued }

drenched in butter
and release him.
There will be
no more mocking,
neither will I
fish here again.

The Closet Naturist

The sun is rising
higher each day,
getting into it's
"I mean business" mode.
A month ago, it
poked up saying:
"This is the best
I can do, learn to
deal with it".
In another month
or two it will
enter into its
"Worship Me"
stage, and
remind me why
I do.

The Fabric Mill

The cotton dust
fills the room
forcing air away.
Up high, near
the flying wheels
cobwebs of lint
mask the motion.
Small children
are best,
then the machines
can be positioned
closer together.
Mind the bobbins
or you'll be docked.
Tie-off too soon,
you'll be docked.
The black iron beast
vomits its flowery
blurred fabric.
The tiny finger
cannot slow the belt,
nor the flywheel,
nor the river, itself.
"There's fifteen yards ruined…
Get that machine running,
and see that she's docked".

Dedicated to the Memory
of the 146 victims of the
Triangle Shirtwaist Factory fire,
mostly women and young girls,
March 25, 1911
New York City

The Horse-Draw

Red snow-fence
separates the spectators
from the
feather-footed
Percherons.
The chains rattle
as the sled
is returned
for the next pair.
An antidote against
the cold,
french fries in
a paper cone,
with vinegar and
too much salt.
The announcer's voice
bounces off the
white church
and returns:
"and now, a local boy
from West Brookfield..."
The Fair has come
to Belchertown.

The Search

Quiet step on
forest ground
ears attuned to
living sound.
High above the
raven sits
lording over
wrens and tits,
breezes filter
through the
the leaves
and spider's silver
threads do weave
amidst the twigs
close to the floor
concealing there
the sacred door
hidden there in
sprigs and pods
that which I seek,
the home of gods.

The Sun

The Sun was angry,
and went to the other
side of the world.
"He can't", I say
"All those people are asleep."
(I stamp my foot)
"Well, he's not here,
and I need him",
"Go take a nap",
my mother says,
"And besides, He's a She."

The Wall
Brimfield, Massachusetts

The stone wall
was gone.
For some childish
reason, I thought
it had settled into
the ground.
Later, older,
I guessed it
had been sold,
rock, stock,
and barrel,
the stones in burlap
sacks to preserve
the lichenous patina
of age.
Perhaps to give
Mayflower provenance
to some trendy
Colonial Reproduction.
New England
for sale.

The Weesit
A Samhain Bed-time Story for Conall & Maggie

In mossy hollows near dampened seeps,
The tiny mortal weesit sleeps
and dreams of eating children small
the laugh and bones and fingers all!

He gnaws the belly-button first,
and stirs the toenails in his wurst,
He weaves bright jackets from the hair
and when he's done there's nothing there!

Only sneaking 'round at night,
Waiting 'til they're tucked in tight,
He slinks from underneath the bed,
Sometimes the foot, sometimes the head.

Blinks his wicked bright red eyes,
Tries not to giggle with surprise,
Then drawn just like the wolf to mutton,
He finds that tiny belly-button!

But not all children disappear,
Else there'd be no grown-ups living here,
Those who close their eyes and sleep
are safe from lurky weesit creep,

But those who cry and carry-on,
Will find surprise before the dawn,

No sleeping child with tousled head
But a tiny jacket on the bed.

2.

So, go to sleep, my beauty child,
Protected from the weesit wild,
The weesit's planning on another,
And will you truly miss your brother?

To Emily

Belle of Amherst, indeed,
White-laced, pampered
and defective.
Not one line
provoked by empty belly.
Nothing to raise
the spirited glass about.
Vacuous mewlings
of the hesitant,
peculiarity posing
as perspicacity.
The polite praise
of pointless paeans
served in precious yore,
now badly translated
mis-understandings
to inflate the past
to suit the present,
treacly, fawning,
a modern generation's
self-aggrandizing
take on The
Empress' New
Clothes.

Tobacco

From atop Mt. Sugarloaf
the netting looks like
square floes in a green
Arctic Sea.
Beneath this white mass
lives tobacco.
The Elite of the Valley thrives
in the cheese-cloth shade.
Once, it was harvested
by children;
Black marker stripe on forearm
to measure the leaf.
Electronic games and
richer parents have ended
those ways.
Now in the humid shade
it is sliced from its stalk
by men who speak
a foreign tongue.

Like a row of gray porpoises
the Ford tractors sit in line
each with its long thin trailer
on mis-matched antique wheels.
The rails are gauged to

{ continued }

fit the lath, which in turn
hold the leaves for
the short journey to
the barn.
Sides open like fish-gills
for light
but failing to catch
the passing breeze.

2.

In choking heat and dust
the laths are hung
and more than a few
reckless hangers
have left the third level
and ended in breathtaking
crash to the dirt.
"Good thing that ain't concrete!"

Here in the dark and the heat
in wry miracle
the dead leaves are cured.
At auction, graded, baled, sold,
then and only then will the farmer
know profit or loss.

Someday, the netting,
the barns, the fine cigar,
will disappear.
I am glad to have seen them, once.

Veteran's Day

A fleshy totem,
the legs of the barstool
support the hero.
"Give me another draft,"
"No, wait, that's what
put me here,"
(laughter).
Spent the entire war
at some obscure base
in New Jersey,
driving Officers from
the airstrip to the billets.
Disabled in inaction.
Too many afternoons
at "The Club", waiting.
Couple of breath-mints
and into the breach.
Good Conduct ribbon
for never getting caught.
There should be a
different word for
the un-blooded, living,
all limbs intact,
but there isn't.

Viet Nam

It's gone, now,
that war.
Jane Fonda in
Support Hose.
Pot bellies on
both sides,
hippies and grunts.
The ugliness superceded
by new reality,
even uglier, if
that could be.
It's hard to
maintain anger
after fifty,
or sorrow.
All the sharp edges
blunted by
memory loss,
rage reduced to
heartburn.
Berets with tiny
emblems celebrate
memorial parades
wrested in beery
combat against
the enemy within.

Why The Sky is Blue
(for Mary)

As denim pants are washed and laid
Or hung outdoors, in air to dry,
Their brilliant blue will quickly fade,
Becoming what we know as "sky".

So when your jeans turn faded gray,
Go purchase new, don't hesitate,
Wash at once and outside lay
Unless you like a sky of gray.

Made in United States
Cleveland, OH
01 April 2025

15734747R00069